Questions and Answers About
SEASHORE
ANIMALS

MICHAEL CHINERY

ILLUSTRATED BY WAYNE FORD, MICK LOATES, AND MYKE TAYLOR

SCHOLASTIC INC.
New York Toronto London Auckland Sydney
Mexico City New Delhi Hong Kong

ISBN 0-439-09964-1

Copyright © 1992, 1994 by Grisewood & Dempsey Ltd. All rights reserved. Published by Scholastic Inc., 555 Broadway, New York, NY 10012, by arrangement with KINGFISHER BOOKS, Grisewood & Dempsey Ltd. SCHOLASTIC and associated logos are trademarks and/or registered trademarks of Scholastic Inc.

12 11 10 9 8 7 6 5 4 3 2   3 4 5/0

Printed in the U.S.A.   14

First Scholastic printing, February 2000

Series editor: Mike Halson
Series designer: Terry Woodley
Designer: Dave West Children's Books
Illustrators: Norman Michael Fahy (p. 38); Wayne Ford (pp. 1–3, 12–13, 17, 27, 29, 32–3); Mick Loates/*Linden Artists* (pp. 8, 14, 20–21, 28, 34); Myke Taylor/*Garden Studio* (pp. 4–7, 9–11, 15–16, 18–19, 22–26, 30–31, 35–37)
Cover illustrations: John Butler

CONTENTS

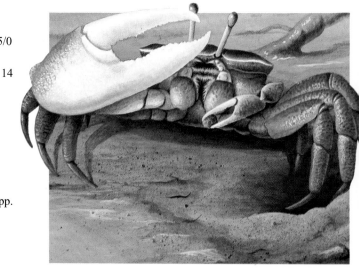

What is life like on the seashore?

Seashores are not all the same. They vary depending on the kind of rock forming the coast. Hard rocks form rugged headlands and rocky beaches, but softer rocks are more likely to produce sandy bays. The animals of these two kinds of seashores are very different. Rocky shores are great for exploring at low tide because hundreds of different animals cling to the rocks and seaweeds. Animals that live on sandy shores have to burrow into the sand when the tide goes out, and this makes the beach look rather empty.

On a rocky shore, seaweeds provide vital food and shelter for many animals. When the tide goes out, most of the animals hide away or fix their shells tightly to the rocks—but where there are rock pools you can watch some seashore creatures moving around in the water.

THE HIGH-WATER MARK

Every time the tide sweeps over the beach it brings with it seaweed and other bits and pieces. This junk stays behind and forms the high-water mark, the highest level reached by the tide before going out. It is a good place to look for small seashore animals.

MANGROVE SWAMPS

Many tropical sea-shores are fringed with small trees called mangroves. These trees all have masses of branching roots, looking like upturned baskets. The roots anchor them in the shifting mud and sand. Mangrove swamps are home to huge numbers of crabs and birds.

Do seagulls always stay by the sea?

Most seagulls are plump white birds with gray wings. They can be found on nearly all the world's seashores, and often follow ships. Seagulls are great scavengers and eat just about anything. They are always screaming at each other and squabbling over food. Some never go to sea at all and spend all their time at dumps and on farms. Huge flocks of gulls follow plows across the fields and snap up the worms and insects that are uncovered. Three of the most common seagulls are shown here.

SEAGULL FACTS

● There are about 45 kinds of seagulls. The great black-backed is the biggest. It is 33 inches long and its wings span 5 feet.

● The smallest gull is the little gull, which is only 11 inches long.

● Seagulls can live for well over 30 years.

The black-headed gull has no dark head feathers in winter—just a dark smudge behind each eye.

Black-headed gulls find plenty of food among the debris at the high-water mark. They live mainly in Europe and Asia.

Seagulls use their webbed feet to paddle around on the surface like ducks, but they rarely dive.

The great black-backed gull of the North Atlantic is as big as a goose. It eats fish, but also takes eggs and chicks from other gulls' nests. It even kills adult birds and rabbits.

Most young gulls are heavily speckled with brown. They may not get their proper adult colors until they are about four years old.

The long, narrow wings are ideal for soaring and gliding in strong wind. Gulls can glide for long periods of time.

The herring gull is a very common gull, found on seashores all round the Northern Hemisphere. Its fluffy chicks look much like those of other gulls. The chicks start to fly when they are about six weeks old.

Hungry chicks peck at the red spot on the adult herring gull's beak, and this makes the adult cough up some food for them.

How does the starfish get its name?

The starfish has no head, only a mouth on the underside of its body. It usually has five arms which give it its star shape. The underside of each arm is covered with little water-filled suckers called tubefeet. These are very strong and they help the starfish to move and to capture food. Shellfish are the starfish's favorite prey.

The starfish moves over the seabed by fixing its suckers to the rocks and then pulling itself forward.

The starfish's strong suckers can easily pull the two halves of a mussel's shell apart. The starfish's mouth then gets to work on the mussel's soft body.

DO YOU KNOW

The starfish has a wonderful ability to repair any injury. If it loses an arm, it simply grows a new one, as you can see here. A torn-off arm can even grow a new body!

Which lizard swims in the ocean?

The marine iguana is the only lizard that regularly takes a dip in the sea. It lives on rocky shores and goes into the sea to browse on seaweeds at low tide. It has partly webbed feet and is a good swimmer, but it does not go far out to sea. It clings to the rocks with its strong claws while feeding, so that the waves do not wash it away. Marine iguanas live only on the Galapagos Islands in the Pacific Ocean.

DO YOU KNOW

Red crabs often scuttle over basking iguanas and sometimes appear to pinch them. The iguanas do not mind, because the crabs are actually pulling blood-sucking ticks from their skin to eat them.

The iguana's sharp teeth are used for tearing the tough seaweeds away from the rocks.

IGUANA FACTS

● The marine iguana is about 3 feet long. Most individuals are plain black or gray.

● When alarmed, the iguana puffs water vapor from its nose—like a fairy tale dragon.

Which animal resembles a flower?

Sea anemones grow on rocks and look more like flowers than animals. Their tentacles, or arms, carry poisonous stings, some of which can be very painful to people. The stings are used to catch fish and other small animals. When the prey has been stung, the arms hold it firmly and push it into the anemone's mouth. You can watch the action by tying a piece of meat to some string and dangling it among the tentacles: it is difficult to pull the meat out again.

ANEMONE FACTS

● The biggest sea anemones are about 2 feet across. They live on the coral reefs of Australia.

● Sea anemones often split in half to produce two new animals.

● Some anemones can live for 100 years.

Plumose anemones have so many fine tentacles that they look like feather dusters. They feed on very small prey.

WALKING ANEMONES

A sea anemone can "walk" over rocks. It leans over (1) and grips the rock with its arms (2). Then it somersaults (3) into a new position (4).

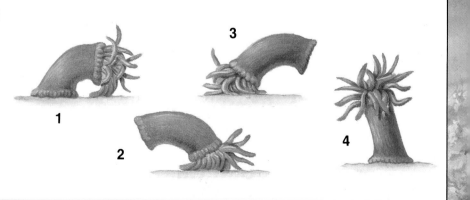

When the tide goes out most kinds of sea anemones, like this attractive red beadlet, pull in their arms and look like blobs of jelly.

DO YOU KNOW

Anemone stings shoot out when touched and quickly kill small animals. Each sting can be used only once, but new ones are always being made.

Trigger

Sting before firing

Sting after firing

Snakelocks anemones cannot pull their long tentacles back into the body. They cannot survive out of the water for long.

The colorful clown fish avoids its enemies by diving into an anemone. Any fish that follows it is stung and eaten, but the anemone does not sting the clown fish.

The mouth of this dahlia anemone is almost closed, but it can open very wide to swallow a fish or other type of prey.

What do crabs like to eat?

Hundreds of different kinds of crabs live on the seashore. They nearly all have a broad, flat shell and a tiny tail tucked up under the rear end. Most crabs have ten legs. The front legs bear large claws and the other eight are used for scuttling sideways over the sand. Crabs eat other animals, alive or dead, and are very fond of dead fish. They often quarrel over food and sometimes fight fiercely with their claws. A crab often loses a claw in one of these battles, but it can grow a new one quite quickly. Large crabs, such as the edible crab, are good to eat and many are caught for food.

 CRAB FACTS

● The biggest crab is the Japanese spider crab. It lives in deep water and its front legs may be 10 feet long.

● The smallest crabs are called pea crabs. Their bodies are less than $\frac{1}{4}$ inch across.

The velvet crab is a good swimmer, thanks to its paddle-shaped back legs.

The masked crab hides in the sand by day, leaving only its two hairy antennae and possibly a claw tip poking out.

— Antennae

The shore crab is a common sight in rock pools. It is like a velvet crab, but has slimmer back legs and is a poor swimmer.

IN THE MANGROVES

Sharp-clawed mangrove crabs climb all over the tangled bushes of the mangrove swamps, while pale-shelled ghost crabs scuttle over the sand.

Mangrove crab

Ghost crabs

DO YOU KNOW

A female crab carries her eggs in a bundle tucked under her tail. The creatures that hatch from the eggs are called larvae and they float to the surface. They do not look like crabs. They change shape several times in the next few months before settling on the seabed and turning into adults.

Crab larvae

Eggs

Edible crabs live on rocky shores. These two are fighting over some mussels and one has lost a claw in the fierce battle.

13

Why do hermit crabs need old shells?

The hermit crab is more like a shrimp than a real crab. It has a long, soft body and protects itself by living in the old shell of a whelk or other sea snail. A pair of strong hooks at its rear end hold the crab safely in the shell. As it gets bigger, the hermit crab moves to a bigger shell. Hermit crabs feed mainly on dead animals.

DO YOU KNOW

Sea anemones often grow on a hermit crab's shell, and the crab may even plant them there. The anemones protect the crab with their stings (see page 10). In return, the crab carries them to new feeding grounds.

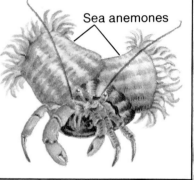

Sea anemones

A small bristleworm often shares the crab's shell. It steals bits of food but does the crab no other harm.

Before moving house, the hermit crab tests the new shell with its claws to see that it is big enough.

The right claw is bigger than the left one and closes the shell when the crab backs in to rest.

Which crab climbs trees?

Robber crabs live on tropical beaches. When they are young they live in the sea, but adults drown if kept underwater for more than a few hours. They feed on dead animals, and can climb trees to get coconuts and other fruit.

Robber crabs use long front claws to climb coconut palms, but it is not true that they throw coconuts to the ground to crack them.

The adult robber crab is about 18 inches long. It has very powerful claws and only four walking legs.

Which fish can walk on mud?

Mudskippers are weird fish that live in coastal swamps in the warmer parts of the world. When the tide goes out they walk and leap over the mud on their armlike front fins. They can even climb trees. They feed on tiny animals in the mud.

The male mudskipper waves the big fin on its back like a flag to attract females.

How is a skimmer's beak special?

Skimmers are well-named birds. They skim over the sea with the lower half of their strange beak in the water ready to scoop up fish and squid. They fish mainly in the evening or at night. The birds shown here are black skimmers from the Atlantic coast of North America. African and Indian skimmers feed mainly in fresh water.

SKIMMER FACTS

- Skimmers are related to gulls. Black skimmers, 20 inches long, are the largest.

- Young skimmers have normal beaks. They pick up their food from the shore.

Skimmers spend the daytime resting on rocks and sandbanks. They can be easily recognized by their oddly shaped beaks.

As soon as the beak touches something in the water it snaps shut. The head is then raised and the prey is swallowed.

The trail of shining bubbles attracts more fish, so the skimmer turns back ready for a second helping.

How does the gray sea eagle catch fish?

The gray sea eagle is a powerful bird of prey living around the coasts of Europe and Asia. It also lives by large lakes and rivers. The eagle scoops fish from the surface with its big talons, but rarely plunges right into the water. Dead sheep also make up part of the eagle's diet in some areas, and it may kill small lambs. The birds build untidy nests in tall trees or on high cliffs. They usually lay two eggs, and the chicks fly when they are about ten weeks old.

DO YOU KNOW

The gray sea eagle is like a pirate. It does not always bother to go fishing itself. It often waits for other birds to fly up with fish and then it chases them until they are exhausted and give up their possessions— just as human pirates did in the past.

Broad wings, about 3 feet across, enable the eagle to carry heavy loads back to its nest.

SURVIVAL WATCH

Gray seas eagles were hunted out of existence in the British Isles 80 years ago, but Norwegian birds taken to Scotland in 1975 are now doing well. More are now being released in Ireland.

The eagle's long toes have sharp spines on them to help the bird grip the fish securely as it flies.

How do sea urchins use their spines?

Sea urchins look like pincushions with the points sticking outward. These spines protect the urchins and help them to walk and dig in the sand. Long water-filled suckers also help with movement. There is a thin shell just under the skin. Most sea urchins feed on seaweeds, which they scrape from the rocks using tough jaws on their underside. Others feed on debris that they collect with their suckers. Some urchins have very short spines that look more like fur. The spines all fall off when the animals die.

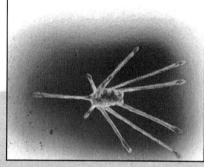

CIDARIS

Cidaris walks over the seabed on its stout spines, which are up to 6 inches long. They are purple at first but turn gray as they age.

The shells of edible sea urchins, up to 6 inches across, make good ornaments. A spine was attached to each pimple in life.

Gulls and other sea-birds often attack rock urchins to get at the soft flesh. The broken shells are often seen on the shore.

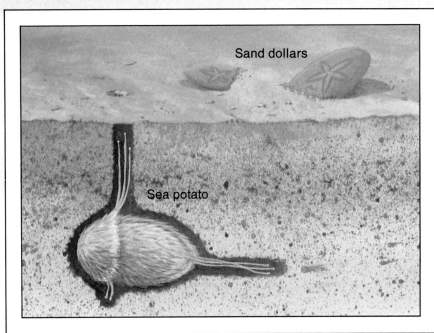

Sand dollars

Sea potato

UNUSUAL URCHINS

Sand dollars are flat, cookie-shaped urchins with short, furlike spines. They eat scraps of food as they plow through the sand. Sea potatoes burrow in the sand. Some of their long suckers collect food, and others reach the surface to allow the urchin to breathe.

Rock urchins live in rock pools. They hide themselves with bits of broken shells and seaweed, held on by their suckers.

 **URCHIN FACTS**

● There are about 600 kinds of sea urchins, ranging from $\frac{1}{2}$ inch to 18 inches in diameter, including their spines.

● The spines of some sea urchins can cause painful wounds if you step on them.

Edible sea urchins normally live below the low-water mark or in rock pools. The soft inner parts are good to eat.

How do mussels stick to rocks?

Deep blue mussel shells cover the rocks on many seashores. The mussels are anchored by tough threads and they never need to move. They feed by straining tiny scraps of food from the water brought in by the tide.

DO YOU KNOW

Many of the mussels we eat come from mussel farms. The mussels grow in long socklike nets that hang in the water. Always surrounded by water and plenty of food, the mussels grow very quickly.

These openings are used to suck in food and water and pump the water out again.

Which shellfish holds treasure?

Oysters are shellfish whose shells are firmly cemented to underwater rocks. They feed by straining food particles from the water. People harvest tons of them each year for food. Oysters are also famous for their pearls, which are used in jewelry.

The upper half of the oyster's crinkly shell is flat and sits on the saucer-shaped lower half like a lid.

DO YOU KNOW

A pearl is produced when a sand grain gets inside the shell and irritates the oyster's skin. The oyster covers the sand with layers of smooth, shiny material and this becomes the pearl.

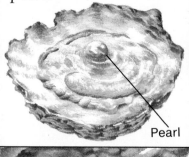

Pearl

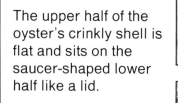

What kind of animal is a limpet?

Limpets are sea snails that live on rocky shores. When the tide comes in they glide over the rocks to graze on the seaweeds. When the tide goes out each limpet returns to its own spot and settles down to rest.

Circular marks show where limpets once lived and their hard shells wore grooves in the rocks.

When out of the water at low tide, the limpet uses its strong muscles to pull the shell tight against the rock. It is extremely hard to pull the animal off.

Which limpet resembles a shoe?

The slipper limpet gets its name because its shell looks rather like a slipper. It is a sea snail, but it does not move around. It fixes itself to stones or other shells around the low-water mark and feeds by filtering tiny food particles from the water.

DO YOU KNOW

Young slipper limpets are all males, but they turn into females as they get older.

Slipper limpets ruin oyster beds by settling on the oysters and stopping them feeding.

Slipper limpets form chains or clusters as big as a man's fist. The smallest and youngest ones in the group are all males.

Why do puffins look funny?

The puffin is famous for its big, colorful beak and its comical, clownlike walk. It looks a bit like a penguin when walking but, unlike penguins, it can also fly. Puffins eat fish and often go far out to sea in the winter. In the summer they breed on the coasts of the North Atlantic and on islands in the Arctic Ocean.

Puffins nest in holes on the tops of cliffs. They often use old rabbit burrows. Females lay just one egg as a rule.

SURVIVAL WATCH

Puffin numbers fell fast in many areas in the 1960s. They have now risen again, especially in the colder regions. These changes may be linked to changes in climate that affect the fish that the puffins eat.

Puffins feed mainly on sand lances. They can carry up to 30 of these slender fish in their big beaks at one time.

The puffin uses its broad webbed feet to change direction and slow itself down when it is flying.

A puffin is about 8 inches high. It flies well, although its plump body looks too heavy for its narrow wings.

How do fanworms gather food?

Vast numbers of worms live on the seashore. They hide under the sand when the tide goes out, but wading birds still find them and eat them. The worms come out to feed when the tide comes in. Many are called fanworms. Instead of hunting, these worms sit still and strain food from the water with fans of feathery tentacles. Most fanworms live in tubes, which often stick out of the sand when the tide is out.

The lugworm spends its entire life in a U-shaped burrow. It sucks mud in through its mouth and passes it out at the other end to form worm casts. The worm digests any scraps of food that it sucks in with the mud.

Lugworm tunnel

Cast

The sand mason (below) glues sand and broken shells together to build a tube. Sabella (on the right) uses much finer sand grains for its tube.

Sabella

Sand-mason

Plug

Serpula fixes its chalky tube to a rock. It hides in its tube when the tide goes out and closes the entrance with a special plug-shaped tentacle.

Honeycomb worms live in large colonies. Their clusters of sandy tubes are fixed to rocks—often in rock pools—and look just like honeycombs.

Why do wading birds have long beaks?

Huge flocks of long-legged wading birds visit the seashores, especially in the winter. They come to feed on the millions of worms, shellfish, and shrimplike creatures that live in the sand, mud, and shallow water along the shore. Many of these birds have very long beaks, with which they feel for prey in the sand or mud. Others catch their food by sweeping their beaks through the water. Many waders are great travelers. They spend the summer in the far north and then fly south to spend the winter by the sea.

The black-winged stilt's extremely long, thin legs enable it to wade in deeper water than other waders to find its food.

The avocet searches for crustaceans in the shallows by sweeping its slightly upturned beak from side to side through the water.

The spoonbill has a spoon-shaped beak, which it sweeps through the water to catch shrimps and other small animals.

The turnstone gets its name because it uses its beak to turn over stones and other objects while it is searching for food.

The redshank scampers over the shore and sweeps its thin beak from side to side through the sand or mud to find food.

The ringed plover usually nests on the shore, where its spotted eggs are well camouflaged among the sand and shingle.

How does a fiddler crab warn off rivals?

The male fiddler crab has one claw very much bigger than the other. The big claw is often brightly colored and it is called a fiddle. The crab uses it like a flag, waving it up and down to tell other males to keep away. The claw is also waved vigorously to attract females. Fiddler crabs live in burrows on seashores, especially in muddy areas near river mouths. They leave their burrows only when the tide goes out.

DO YOU KNOW

Each of the many kinds of fiddler crab has its own signaling system. Females are attracted only to males of their own kind.

Some fiddlers make sounds by rubbing the large claw against a row of teeth on the front of the shell.

The female is less colorful than the male. She has two normal claws and uses them both to get food from the mud.

The color of the crab's shell is always changing. It is particularly bright when the male is waving to a female.

Fiddler crabs stay near their burrows. When the tide comes in each crab goes into its burrow and closes the entrance with a lump of mud.

The crabs feed by picking up sand or mud in their small claws and licking tiny animals and other food from it.

When do barnacles open?

Barnacles form crusty white coverings on many seaside rocks. They look dead when the tide is out, but they open up to feed when it returns. Young barnacles swim in the sea for a time before settling down.

The tentlike shell opens underwater and feathery legs comb tiny scraps of food from the water.

DO YOU KNOW

Barnacles are related to crabs, although an adult barnacle does not look like a crab at all. A young barnacle (below) looks almost like a baby crab until it settles down and forms its shell.

Which animal digs its own tomb?

The piddock is a shellfish that uses the spiny front end of its shell to tunnel slowly into underwater rocks. It can live for a long time in its tunnel, but it can never turn around and tunnel out again.

The piddock filters scraps of food from the water that it sucks in through long tubes called siphons.

The two halves of the piddock's shell twist from side to side like a drill, so that it can bore into soft rock.

27

Why is the weever fish dangerous?

Weever fish burrow in sand with just their poison spines exposed. They live in shallow water near the coasts of Europe and Africa and eat shrimps and other small animals.

The spines on the weever's back cause a lot of pain if they are stepped on.

Which fish clings to rocks?

Gobies are small fish that live in coastal areas all over the world. Several kinds are common in rock pools. They have two fins on the top of the body, the front one being rather spiny. The lower fins form a sucker.

? DO YOU KNOW

The world's smallest fish is a type of goby. It is only $\frac{5}{8}$ inch long.

Some gobies use empty seashells as nests for their eggs. Male gobies always guard the eggs.

The goby's sucker, formed when the lower fins are joined together, enables the fish to cling to rocks. This stops it from being swept away by the current.

Where do guillemots lay their eggs?

Guillemots live all round the northern seas and feed on fish and crustaceans that they usually catch by swimming underwater. They breed in noisy colonies on narrow cliff ledges. Each female lays one egg on the bare rock.

The guillemot's pointed egg rolls round in a circle if it is knocked—and does not fall off the ledge.

How long can a cormorant hold its breath?

Cormorants are fish-eating birds and they can chase their prey underwater for up to a minute. There are several kinds, found nearly all over the world.

? DO YOU KNOW

The droppings of South American guanay cormorants are used as fertilizer.

In some places anglers tie cormorants to long lines and use them to catch fish.

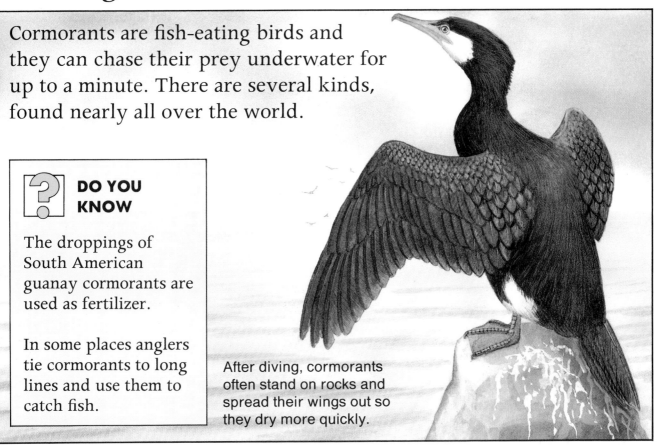

After diving, cormorants often stand on rocks and spread their wings out so they dry more quickly.

Where would you find a scarlet ibis?

The scarlet ibis is one of the world's most colorful birds. Big flocks live in the mangrove swamps along the coasts and rivers of the Gulf of Mexico and the Caribbean. It uses its long, curved beak to catch fish and to dig for crabs and other small animals in the mud. Ibises build large, untidy nests of sticks.

Scarlet ibises look like showers of red confetti when they arrive to roost in the mangroves in the evening. They flap their wings in unison, as if they were all tied together.

The young scarlet ibis has black and white feathers. It does not get its brilliant red coat until it is over a year old.

What is the name of the smallest penguin?

The fairy penguin is the world's smallest penguin. It lives on rocky coasts in New Zealand and Australia. It feeds on fish in the coastal waters by day, and comes ashore to sleep at night. Unlike most other penguins, it does not form crowded colonies, and each pair likes to nest alone.

Penguins are built for life in cold water, but they do not all live in the Antarctic. Cold ocean currents enable jackass penguins to live in South Africa, while Galapagos penguins live as far north as the equator.

Galapagos penguin

Jackass penguin

Fairy penguins build their nests in caves or burrows where the chicks are sheltered from the sun.

Fairy penguins are about 16 inches high. Because of their color they are also called blue penguins.

SURVIVAL WATCH

Fairy penguins are much less common than they used to be. Many have been killed by dogs, cats, and other animals brought over by European settlers. They are also often run over by cars. Most of the remaining penguins now live on remote coasts and islands.

What are the two main kinds of seashell?

Seashells are the cases of soft-bodied animals called mollusks or shellfish. When the animals die, the empty shells are washed up on the beach. There are thousands of different kinds, belonging to two main groups—sea snails and bivalves. Sea snails have coiled shells like land snails. Bivalve shells have two halves hinged together. Sea snails have mouths full of small, sharp teeth, with which they eat seaweeds or other animals. Bivalves strain small scraps of food from the water.

 **DO YOU KNOW**

Colorful seashells, like the tiger cowrie shown below, have long been used as ornaments and for making jewelry. In some places shells were once used as money. The chinalike cowrie shells were the favorites because they are smooth and easy to handle.

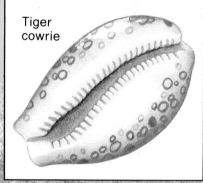

Tiger cowrie

Buried in the sand, the tellin uses two long siphons to suck in rubbish from the seabed and pump out what it doesn't eat.

The cockle only has short siphons, and it buries itself just below the surface. It sucks in water and strains food from it.

Cockles and most other bivalves burrow in mud and sand with the aid of a muscle called the foot.

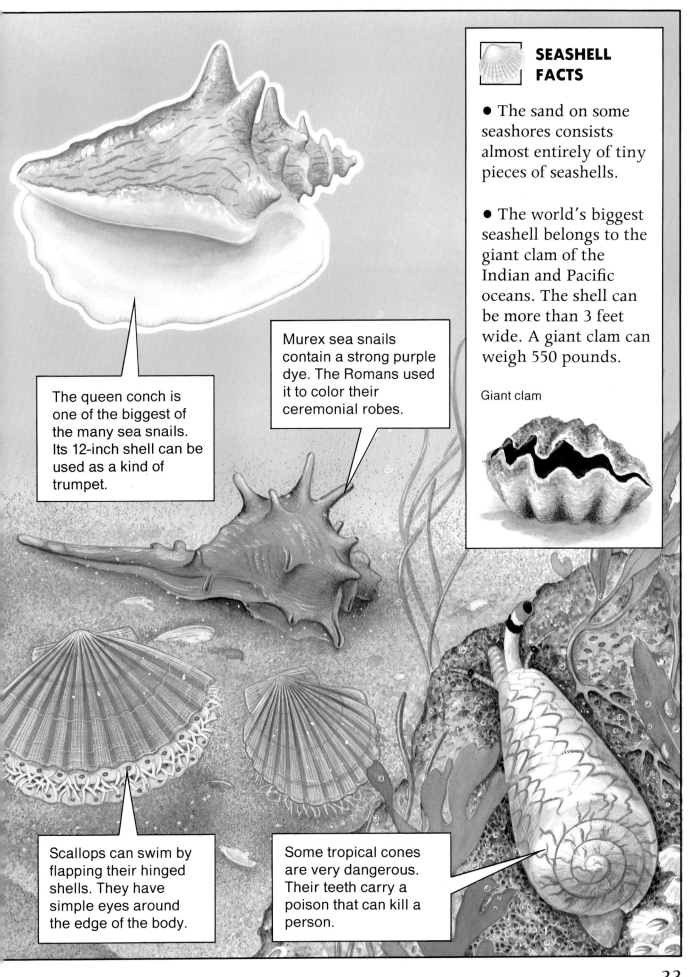

- The sand on some seashores consists almost entirely of tiny pieces of seashells.

- The world's biggest seashell belongs to the giant clam of the Indian and Pacific oceans. The shell can be more than 3 feet wide. A giant clam can weigh 550 pounds.

Giant clam

The queen conch is one of the biggest of the many sea snails. Its 12-inch shell can be used as a kind of trumpet.

Murex sea snails contain a strong purple dye. The Romans used it to color their ceremonial robes.

Scallops can swim by flapping their hinged shells. They have simple eyes around the edge of the body.

Some tropical cones are very dangerous. Their teeth carry a poison that can kill a person.

Where do sea slugs live?

Sea slugs, like their land-living cousins, are really snails without shells. Some sea slugs live close to the shore, but others live in very deep water. Some spend all their lives swimming in the open ocean. Sea slugs include some of the most colorful of all sea creatures. Most sea slugs feed on other small animals, including sea anemones and sponges, but there are some vegetarian kinds that only feed on seaweeds.

DO YOU KNOW

A few kinds of sea slugs eat small sea anemones without making them fire their stings (see page 11). The sea slugs store the stings in their bodies and fire them at their own enemies. Instead of having a tasty meal, a predator gets a mouthful of stings.

The sea lemon is one of the commonest sea slugs. It feeds on small sponges and can often be found in rock pools. It is 3 inches long.

The gray sea slug is up to 3 inches long and eats sea anemones. It lays its eggs in long white ribbons.

The sea lemon breathes by means of these tufts of leaflike gills. It can pull them into its body.

These wormlike flaps take oxygen from the water for breathing. They may also carry unfired stings from the slug's prey (see above).

What is the spiny lobster's other name?

Spiny lobsters, or crayfish, live in rocky places—usually below low-tide level. Up to 18 inches long, they are a popular food. They lack the big pincers of true lobsters.

The spiny lobster has no big claws. It defends itself by lashing out with its long, spiny antennae.

How do horseshoe crabs look for food?

Horseshoe crabs, or king crabs, live on sandy beaches in the warmer parts of the world. They can swim on their backs, but spend most of their time digging in the sand in search of worms and other small animals.

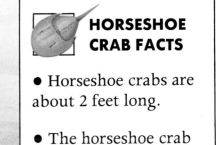
HORSESHOE CRAB FACTS

● Horseshoe crabs are about 2 feet long.

● The horseshoe crab is not really a crab. It is more closely related to land-dwelling spiders and scorpions.

The spiky tail pushes the animal along, and also turns it the right way up if it is over-turned by waves.

How do shrimps and prawns swim?

Shrimps and prawns are related to crabs, but they are much slimmer and usually swim well. They have five pairs of legs, with pincers on the front ones and sometimes on others as well. The back half of the body carries small, feathery limbs that are used as paddles when swimming. The tail fan can be opened out and used as a flipper.

These animals eat whatever they can find on the seabed. We eat a lot of them ourselves. Live ones are mostly brown, but they turn pink when cooked.

DO YOU KNOW

Chameleon prawns live in rock pools, but they are hard to see because they change color to match their backgrounds—just like real chameleons. They are sand-colored on sand, but green or brown if crawling on seaweed.

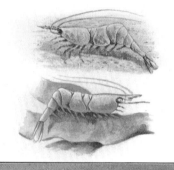

The common prawn is up to 4 inches long and can be easily recognized by the pointed, sawlike ridge on the top of its head.

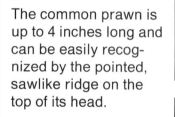

Prawns like rocky areas and you can often see them walking or swimming in rock pools. They use the front two pairs of legs, which have little pincers on them, to pick up scraps of food.

The female prawn glues more than 2,000 eggs to her swimming legs and carries them until they hatch a few weeks later.

The Norway lobster likes muddy areas and does not often come to the shore. It uses its big pincers for defense and collects food with the smaller ones. The Norway lobster's flesh is called scampi.

The Norway lobster is up to 6 inches long and does not swim. Its rather flat body is designed for crawling over sand and mud.

The skeleton shrimp, or ghost shrimp, is not a real shrimp at all. It clings to seaweed and grabs small animals with its claws.

The common shrimp looks like a prawn, but it has no toothed ridge on its head and its front legs are much stouter. The shrimp hides in the sand by day and hunts for animal food at night.

Why are seashore animals in danger?

Many seashores are littered with plastic bottles and ropes and other trash, but the most serious problem is oil. Huge ships carry oil across the oceans, and if there is an accident thousands of tons of oil may leak into the sea. Tides wash the oil onto the shore and, as well as spoiling the beaches for swimming, it destroys the seashore plants and animals. We can clean a sandy beach quite quickly, but nature needs many years to clean the rocks and replace the lost seaweeds and animal life.

SAVING SEABIRDS

The worst casualties of oil spills are puffins and other seabirds that have to dive through the oil to catch their fish. Covered with the slimy oil, they die if they get no help. Luckily, we can clean them with special detergents or soap. As long as the birds have not swallowed too much oil they will survive. They are kept in captivity until their feathers have regained their natural waterproofing—and then they are released.

Oil leaking from a damaged tanker forms a thick black sheet on the surface of the water. Detergents help to break this up, while people and machines struggle to remove the sticky oil from the beach.

Useful words

Antenna One of the feelers of crabs and their relatives that help the animals to pick up smells and to find their way around.

Bivalve The name given to any of the seashells, such as cockles and mussels, that are in two parts with a hinge along one edge.

Camouflage The way in which animals avoid the attention of their enemies by resembling their surroundings or blending in with them. The animals are then not easy to recognize.

Coast The edge of the land, where it meets the sea.

Crustacean Any member of the crab and lobster group of animals—hard-shelled creatures with lots of legs.

Eurasia The name given to the large land mass that consists of the continents of Europe and Asia.

Fin Any of the limbs or other flaps that fish use for swimming.

Gill The breathing organ of fish, crustaceans, and many other water-dwelling animals. It takes life-giving oxygen from the water flowing over it.

High-water mark The line of debris left on the shore at high-tide level.

Larva The name given to a young animal, particularly a crustacean or an insect, that is noticeably different in shape from the adult.

Marine Concerning the sea.

Mollusk Any animal of the group containing slugs, snails, and bivalves. Mollusks have soft bodies and no legs, and most are enclosed in a hard shell.

Scavenger An animal that feeds mainly on dead matter—especially one that clears up the remains of another animal's meal.

Shellfish The name given to various hard-shelled sea creatures, especially cockles and mussels and their relatives. Crabs and other crustaceans are also commonly known as shellfish.

Shingle Coarse gravel and pebbles, up to about 2 inches across, found on the upper parts of the seashore.

Siphon A tube through which many mollusks suck water into their bodies for breathing and feeding. Many have a second siphon for pumping the water out again.

Tentacle A soft, fingerlike projection that is found near the mouth of many animals, including sea anemones. Tentacles are normally used for catching food.

Tide The regular rise and fall of sea level, which floods and then uncovers the seashore twice every day.

Tropical To do with the tropics— the warm areas of the world on each side of the equator.

Wader The name given to various long-legged birds that feed on marshland and in shallow water at the edge of the sea

Index